C000107855

chengyu:
chinoiserie

First published 2020 by The Hedgehog Poetry Press

Published in the UK by
The Hedgehog Poetry Press
5, Coppack House
Churchill Avenue
Clevedon
BS21 6QW

www.hedgehogpress.co.uk

ISBN: 978-1-913499-04-4

Copyright © Leung Rachel Ka Yin 2020

The right of Leung Rachel Ka Yin to be identified as the author of this work has been asserted in accordance with the Copyright, Designs and Patents Act 1988.

All rights reserved. No part of this publication may be reproduced, stored in or introduced into a retrieval system, or transmitted in any form, or by any means (electronic, mechanical, photocopying, recording or otherwise) without prior written permissions of the publisher. Any person who does any unauthorised act in relation to this publication may be liable for criminal prosecution and civil claims for damages.

9 8 7 6 5 4 3 2 1

A CIP Catalogue record for this book is available from the British Library.

Cover art © Elliana Esquivel

for SW, my muse

Contents

chengyu: chinoiserie

by

Leung Rachy Ka Yin

dead heart, prostrate: *i'm all yours* (死心塌地)

-for sheng wei-

what colour,
when the heart dies?
and who
and where
and why does it sigh like the wind did
the night i decided to love you?

at once, my suppleness left me.
tender, like a soul leaving
through a wide-open mouth.
i am a swimming sluice,
in a net of slender bones.
oh! how i long for your soft,
for jellyfish kiss but day by day
i am barren in my sleep,
waking to the fresh ache of birth purpling
my veins until your touch.

maybe i am the inside of a drum.
the pious mother of your shapeless children,
hallowing, as the word became flesh,
(*yet fleshless, yet wordless*)
my neck to the blades of your shoulder,
my heart red and sweet martyrdom.

feeling cavity opens for the first time: *love awakens* (情竇初開)

-for lin-

fresh, greening buds between her fingers,
nipped in early spring and curling
up upon itself. before the sun rises
she knows only brick upon brick of red bruising
what would have been bright,
clean edelweiss.

she wonders of what secrets hide under their
small white skirts
what promises of things
that spring will bring
to her parched lips

and where eden lies
she does not know. *riverrun,*
riverrun, dawn comes with
riverrun past Eve and Adam's,
skin haze on
mouth, urgent and
bright like his pulse, her
salt-sweet homunculus.

God teaches weakness,
meekness and to be
lesser than less. but even
in the soft surrender of his pertinent summer, the
Sun hanging high in the stainless blue, she
finds herself thinking up a tempest,
some taxidermy of her tongue on
the young girl's vestal navel.

so, *forgive me, Father:*
hail Mary, full of grace...
(this is when the dusky pastel falls a'sleeping)
...blessed art thou amongst Women...
(through pores and cracks her
heady sea-foam maiden)
...the fruit of thy womb...
(plump and slithering her caress)
...the hour of our death.
(till nightfall on her knees,
doing penance for her sins).

sea oath, mountain treaty: *till the end of time* (海誓山盟)

-for sheng wei-
-inspired by habitation, by Margaret Atwood-

the day you left home with a one-way ticket,
was the day i told you that
walking on air felt
the same as treading water.

the day you waded into the ocean,
was the day i clawed around for some vestigial
memory of fire,
and not remembering,
sat in the darkness, turned
skyward.

many a day you watched as the
sun began and
ended, Genesis upon
Genesis and sleep thick
upon liquid sleep, and far
i take on the colour of
your shadow, or your limpid eyes,
becoming a hymn of your strained
breathing
on the telephone.

at night i dream of you drifting,
my lover gold and rippling sea,
like a child, like my song;
but stirring, i return to the
hum and cry of this brief world, and
bare, and cold.

love is not
a house or even a tent
it is before that, and colder:

the edge of the forest, the edge
of the whitewashed outhouse where
someone with a nail, scrapes dimly in the paint;
LOVE IS NOT A VICTORY MARCH.

where having fought, and lost,
you make for yourself a fragility,
a soft and quivering precious
it is the
sea and the sea and the
mountain and the mountain
swimming in your pocket,
awaiting creation to begin.

paper drunk, gold bewitched: *the new americana* (紙醉金迷)

-for laurice-

"Then wear the gold hat, if that will move her;
If you can bounce high, bounce for her too,
Till she cry "Lover, gold-hatted, high-bouncing lover,
I must have you!" -Thomas Parke D'Invilliers

love, sing me a daisy, a fistful a penny
rain fever sweet in your riotous twenties
star-spangled, light-speckled, glitter aplenty

love, sing me a maqam* and i promise to cry
you tears of black gold, till you will have me, high
on your stones, breathe in my bones, my bones, bone-dry.

you had your lush, lush rush, your roaring nights
of brazen swirling silken shirts, wet, stretched tight
over my heart of cold, vulgar, veblen-esque delight

and i, since you have left, have been scratching at it
a scab- a little, jaded, cynical something unfit to skip to stop,
buried deep in greenback kisses

love, sing me a song- anything-
drown me in my pool of roses,
of glimmering silver rings,
in your voice full of money, of snapped fairy wings

ain't it a kitschy world, love,
all that glitters is not gold.
just like me,
look closely,
guldet blev til sand.

*maqam: the system of melodic modes used in traditional Arabic music
*guldet blev til sand: Swedish, "gold turned into sand", from the musica Kristina från Duvemåla (1995)

a long night is fraught with many a dream: *before morning comes* (夜長夢多)

-for racor-

i am crossing over
in the dark.
over
these dream-infested waters,
my eyes ticking, ticking like the
black time and marching hand
hurrying us to comely grave-
we must hasten! hasten
along the bendy silence where
midwinter the sun like us in leaden sleep
hides,
i must cross over
in the dark with my goggles on
dodging mares in the night
before
mourning comes for me.

the house of dried fish: *dreaming and waterless* (枯魚之肆)

-for vanessa-

lend me
the thrill, the terrible thrill
of a waterless fish.

fresh and desperate,
and eyes and fins and gills
palpitating a silence, wide-open

on the tarmac, dreaming
of quicksand and molasses and road-kill,
gulping, in the fragrant swathes of sun.

nothing of how lidless,
and permeable and defenseless, and ill
it feels, in a moist, feverish skin,

clutching but a swelling tear, salt-tinged,
from eyes wide shut, that spills
as it lies,
dreaming and waterless.

drunk on life, dreaming of death: *living life as if befuddled* (醉生夢死)

-for june-

i cannot capture this colour of sky,
this damned smear from
paper slit, gaping giddy
Bolshevik daddy.
it's the devil's rouge, he took his thumb
and blotted God out.

i am confused.
i think
my blueness is a shade of red
like a baby bleeds
and stretches its diaphanous skin,
ballooning through
the camera's one glassy eye.

it sees you,
lover boy,
my sharpest jealousy.
i will forget your name, too,
your name which for thousands of days
sleeps glowing on my tongue
leaves
nothing, nothing,
nothing of its urgent fluorescence.

fuck me colourless,
drink me fast.
'til my life will exit reticently,
drained of the sun's fire.

the flowers of the heart bloom wildly: *elation* (心花怒放)

-for cj-

when in the morning
i wake to
your touch and lucent sigh
in the
folds of me,
soft kindling all the
rage
and rage within,
i listen to my soul's turnings
and gossamer
hummings,
a throbbing pulse on
open sea.

i should want to bury
myself,
head
in shoulder
and
soft
on soft.
my heart sings
of things
that dream of flying,
and flowers a'bloom:
love-in-a-mist,
forget-me-not.

in sleep
and wordless, you
and me,
eye on quiet eye,
yet gentle,
holding the vivid colours
of gaze, ever and ever
under some sliver of blue and blue
sky.

caped with the stars, wearing the moon: *lune* (披星戴月)

-for victor-

I

sink, sink deep
and
carve a niche into my head
fish scales falling
fall
fall the way
still-green leaves
fall like rain
wind,
wind,
sky
grey

a concrete lightness
simmering stones and
stale week-old tea bags
stuck
a splinter
a lancet
a three-inch tarantula in my side

i cannot look you in
the eye, the eye, the eye.

II

it sings
it stops
it threatens to turn me inside out
from the throat
from the seams
in.

my
my
my
fingers you were holding as we
navigate the crowded platform
in the warm wind,
white light
on the train
kite-running from the smashed window-panes
a fishing line
a telephone line
a flying
crescent ridge, half lune

never the sun but always the moon.

it sighs in technicolour
spin, spin, spinning.

a trickle of water runs long: *always* (細水長流)

-for gladys-

in this sweet summer-spring, you become
this languid body of mine,
this languid body of water, you
become
a lazing creek
run-skipping by my house on its way
to elysium.

this year barefoot,
like the last,
your laughs will ring silvery as the morn.
you will trip-skim
over bright pebbles and pool
amongst the slender reeds, kissing my
ten
white
toes.

today,
we bathe in the syrupy noonlight, wading,
and you giggle and bubble
in whisper-breeze,
assuring me that you are
very real, and very in love with me.

at that, a birth of tadpoles frolick, capricious.
the dragonflies dip for a cool drink
and you gurgle in round vowels of
soft joy.

i will pray that tomorrow brings
rain,
or tears,
to grow your blossoms,
to soothe your sharp edges and
that some drops will ripple your lucid face
to wash you of sorrows so
you can remember to sing to me, so long
as your trickling heart and fountain song.

speak of love in small whispers: *first* (細語訴情)

-for sheng wei-

if you could give to me the first whisper
that flits in splinters from the lips and
still lies long with
grief upon your cheek-
the one that hesitates and
sighs to start again
to
tell of parted halves and
quartered quarters but slumbering
forgets to rewind and
repeat.

if you could give to me the first pain
and the second that rushes through
the windy lanes in chorus to salute the
heart in its casket,
remembering the name in
the eye of your
aching dream-
perhaps, then,
you will drown in its terrible
sillage,
you my one most
tender,
tongueless theme.

if you could give the first falling to me,
the first falling from a
great height after which you will
find yourself alive at last-
gliding with such irrationality through
feverish spring,
and sweet, and fresh perhaps
your blood will sing and
the moon, will for once,
arch towards the looking-glass.

and now
i will give to you my
end,
my one and final true,
therefore-
song and roar and murmur
(my voice)
to whom refuge bright my soul
belongs
through and through and
through.

Acknowledgements

I gratefully acknowledge the editors and publishers of the following publications in which some of these poems first appeared: *Mingled Voices 3: The International Proverse Poetry Prize Anthology 2018*, *ASH Michaelmas 2018*.

My greatest thanks to Kayo Chingonyi for selecting "lune" as as Special Commendation in the Oxford Brookes International Poetry Competition 2018 (EAL Category).

About Leung Rachel Ka Yin

Leung Rachel Ka Yin is a student at the University of Oxford from the vibrant city of Hong Kong. Born and raised in the Pearl of the Orient, which has had great influence on her writing, she attended Diocesan Girls' School and Li Po Chun United World College.

She has been a fervent lover of poetry, since a young age, starting out as a Hong Kong Budding Poet at the Hong Kong Academy of Gifted Education, and going on to earn Second Place in the Young Laureate's Award (national literacy competition) with her poetry.

Her works have been published or featured in various journals and publications, such as the Proverse Poetry Prize (Single Poems) 2018 Anthology: Mingled Voices 3, ASH (the termly literary journal of the Oxford University Poetry Society), Cha: An Asian Literary Journal, Hong Kong Free Press, HK01, The Cherwell and Mekong Review.

Two of her poems have been awarded Second Place and Special Commendation in the Oxford Brookes International Poetry Competition, one of which is included in this pamphlet.

She was formerly the Online Fiction Director of Isis Magazine, the longest-running student magazine in the UK; and is a Poetry Reader at The Adroit Journal and Poetry Editor at Figure of Speech, TRACK//FOUR and Sandpiper.

Rachel is passionate about feminism and mental health, as well as issues surrounding language, culture and identity. Aside from writing and editing poetry, she also writes and edits non-fiction articles on style at PHASER, Oxford University's Music and Style Magazine, where she is Deputy Editor.

Her writings and publications can be found on her website: rachelkayin.com.